"Farmgirls, those
of us living or
longing to live
in the country,
are just about
everybody I know,
girls anyhow."

– MARYJANE BUTTERS

ISBN: 1-933662-01-8

This book may be ordered by mail from the publisher.
Please include $3.50 for postage and handling.

Please support your local bookseller first!

Books published by Cider Mill Press Book Publishers are available
at special discounts for bulk purchases in the United States
by corporations, institutions, and other organizations.
For more information, please contact the publisher.

Cider Mill Press Book Publishers
"Where good books are ready for press"
12 Port Farm Road
Kennebunkport, Maine 04046

Visit us on the web!
www.cidermillpress.com

Design by: Carol Hill
Typography: Filosofia, Dearest, Typewriter Oldstyle

Printed in China
1 2 3 4 5 6 7 8 9 0
First Edition

contents

Ladies Home
JOURNAL
The Magazine Women Believe In
September 1943 • Fifteen Cents
WOMEN WAR WORKERS
This torch burion is dedicated by the
Government to women workers filling
men's jobs, on farms, in shops, offices
and public service, for the duration.
Mousie
COMPLETE NOVEL
By Viña Delmar
WHAT'S A FARM GIRL?

what's a farmgirl?

If you bought this book or received it as a gift, you're probably a farmgirl already, or at least a "closet farmgirl." On the book tour for my recently-released book, *MaryJane's Ideabook, Cookbook, Lifebook For the Farmgirl in All of Us* (billed as "aprons galore on tour"), I met lots of farmgirls, even in the cities I visited! (Now, I'm a stay-at-home, end-of-the-road "country" farmgirl if ever there was one, but given my kids are grown and able to help me run my farm — bringing with them spouses to add to the number of willing hands — it hasn't hurt me one bit to venture out into the world.)

And the number of farmgirls tucked away from here to there and everywhere? Goodness, I stopped counting, but meeting so many sure did help me flesh out my definition of farmgirl.

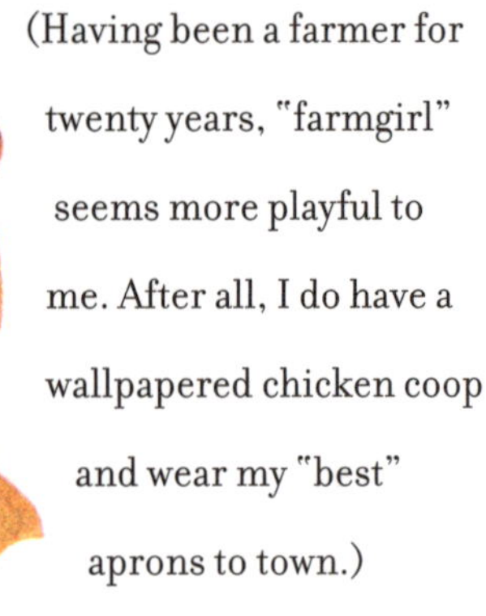

(Having been a farmer for twenty years, "farmgirl" seems more playful to me. After all, I do have a wallpapered chicken coop and wear my "best" aprons to town.)

So at this point, if you still giggle with your

girlfriends, crave vine-ripened tomatoes (love apples), potatoes (earth apples), or homemade apple pie, you're a farmgirl in *my* book!

 Oops ... there *is* one thing you should know to qualify for farmgirl status, and that's the difference between hay and straw. If you're a city chick and you know this, why, you can impress even the likes of my Farm Aid hero, Willie Nelson. Hay is packed with protein. An animal can live on it. But if you're thinking about getting a job buckin' "hay" bales, see if you can find one buckin' "straw" bales instead. Remember the straw man on the Wizard of Oz? Well, he had air for brains. Straw is lighter than hay. It's merely the stalk of the plant and doesn't include the nutritious top. But once you get your garden growing, straw mulch is indispensable, and for farm animals, straw bedding is essential. There now. You can pass muster with the misters.

Us farmgirls everywhere, we're growing exponentially

and we're unleashing our hands-on creativity in time-honored ways (and yes, that includes the Internet, since I host a most amazing chatroom called the "Farmgirl Connection"). "I can do this!" is what I'm hearing. From organic salads to die for, to farm-style family celebrations, to building our own houses and barns, to owning our own farms, to toxin-free housekeeping, to homemade hand-stitched gifts and even clothespin dolls, healthier living in general and simple pleasures in particular are making a comeback.

In my travels, I did not meet one single woman who didn't have a nurturing side to her, making her capable of great love, the kind that loves a child or a chicken (a pet that helps with breakfast), a plant ... anything that grows, really. But there is just one more thing I think us farmgirls need to pitch in for, and that's to remember to go beyond our families, meaning we ought also to love our neighbors (or at least know them — you know, that one right next door) and to think about how making even the tiniest positive change in our own lives is the only way (and I want to emphasize this emphatically) — the ONLY way — to improve our world.

Purl one, purl two are knitting terms (knitting is farmgirl style at its best and has made a ferocious comeback). So purl one (smile when it's hard), purl two (laugh extra hard), and purl three (you'll see).

"Nationally, women are the largest — and fastest growing — group of people buying small farms. Some figures indicate that in 10 years, 75 percent of American farmland will be owned by women."

– PETER MILLER,
Vermont Farm Women

farmgirl up your life

For rural women, necessity is the mother of invention. Using our imaginations and making-do is just part of the job. But being an inventor isn't difficult. If you stop to think about it, you've probably invented a long list of household items by now. Remember that clever coat-hanger hook you devised to hold your reading lamp for bedtime books? When it comes to being the mother of invention, don't think only in terms of needle and thread, nuts and bolts. My mother used to say to me, "Where's your mother wit?" when my imagination stalled. She was saying, "Go for it! You can find a way." Old-fashioned farmgirl common sense and gumption can solve most any problem, fill any void. The next time something isn't quite right in your life, put your thinking cap on. Imagination is more important than knowledge.

farmgirl
recipes
for life, love & family
FOR LIFE LOVE & FAMILY

quintessential quinoa

Quinoa (pronounced Keen-wah) is an almost perfect food in my book. It's a tall, stunning plant that's easy to grow. Thought of as a grain, it's really the fruit of an herb plant that is a distant cousin to spinach. It's no wonder the ancient Incas called quinoa the "mother grain." It's certainly a staple in my life. Unlike other "grains," quinoa has the perfect balance of amino acids, making it a complete protein. What I love most about quinoa is how fast it cooks — fifteen minutes. When done, it has a soft, delicate presence on the tongue without ever being mushy or starchy. If you haven't tried quinoa, you'll want to start with the recipes I've included in this section. Beyond these, let your farmgirl creativity be your guide.

FOR LIFE LOVE & FAMILY

FARMGIRL RECIPES

breakfast quinoa

1 1/2 cups water

3/4 cup quinoa

1/3 cup golden raisins (or any dried fruit)

1/2 teaspoon cinnamon

1/2 teaspoon sea salt

2 teaspoons flax seeds

1/2 cup walnuts, chopped or halved

1. In a medium saucepan, blend together water, quinoa, raisins, cinnamon, and salt.
2. Bring to a boil. Reduce heat to a simmer, cover, and cook for 15 minutes.
3. Remove from heat. Stir in flax seeds and walnuts. Serve immediately.

Yield: four 1/2-cup servings

fruit & herb quinoa

1 1/2 cups water

3/4 cup quinoa

1 small jalapeño pepper, whole

3 tablespoons oil (olive, flax seed, or hemp)

1 tablespoon red onion, chopped

2 tablespoons fresh sage, chopped (2 tsp. dried)

2 tablespoons fresh basil, chopped (2 tsp. dried)

2 tablespoons fresh parsley, chopped (2 tsp. dried)

1/4 cup dried blueberries, raisins or craisins

1. In a medium saucepan, blend together water, quinoa, and whole jalapeño pepper.
2. Bring to a boil. Reduce heat to a simmer, cover, and cook for 15 minutes.
3. Remove from heat. Stir in oil, onion, herbs, and blueberries. Serve immediately.

Yield: four 1/2-cup servings

FOR LIFE LOVE & FAMILY

FARMGIRL RECIPES

rosehip tea with milk

3 cups water
1 cup fresh rosehips
1 cup milk
1 teaspoon almond extract

1. In a medium saucepan, bring water to a boil. Place rosehips in a 4-cup measuring cup or medium bowl. Pour hot water over and let steep for 10 minutes.
2. Strain tea, and stir in milk and almond extract. Reheat.

Yield: four 1-cup servings

FARM GIRL RECIPES

farmgirl
apple pie
FOR LIFE LOVE & FAMILY

cast iron apple pie

5 pounds medium firm apples (try using several
    different cooking varieties), peeled, cored,
    and cut into 1/4 inch-thick wedges

1/4 cup lemon juice

1 teaspoon lemon zest

1 1/3 cups plus 2 tablespoons sugar, divided

1 teaspoon ground cinnamon

1/2 teaspoon ground nutmeg

1/2 teaspoon sea salt

3 tablespoons butter, diced

2 tablespoons half-n-half

(to use a regular 9-inch pie plate, cut above
ingredients in half)

1. Preheat oven to 400°F.
2. In a large bowl, toss the apples with lemon juice
and zest.
3. In a separate bowl, mix the 1 1/3 cups sugar,

cinnamon, nutmeg, and salt. Sprinkle over the
apples and toss to coat.

4. Place one prepared crust (next page) into a No. 8
(10-inch) cast iron skillet. Spoon in filling; dot the
top with butter.

5. Drape the second prepared crust over the filling.
Seal top and bottom crust edges together and crimp
decoratively.

6. Cut slits in top crust, brush with half-n-half, and
sprinkle with 2 tablespoons sugar.

7. Transfer pie to baking sheet and cover the edges
with foil.

8. Bake for 40 minutes. Reduce heat to 325°F;
remove foil and bake for 30–35 minutes or until
crust is golden brown.

Yield: one 10-inch pie

"I made your pie for the 4th of July and it became legendary in seconds! The crust was almost like a butter cookie, and I loved how the filling turned out. Oh my, I was so proud of that pie!"
— JENNIFER, ST. PETERSBURG, FLORIDA

butter cookie pie crust

2 ½ cups flour
½ teaspoon salt
1 cup cold butter, diced
1 teaspoon sugar
5 tablespoons cold water

Sift together flour, sugar, and salt in a bowl.
Using a pastry blender or fork, cut butter into dry
ingredients until mixture resembles coarse meal.
Sprinkle cold water evenly over surface (1 tablespoon
at a time); stir until moistened. Shape dough into two
disks, wrap in parchment paper, and chill 1 hour or
freeze up to 3 weeks.

Yield: two 9 to 10-inch single pie crusts or one
double pie crust

pear and garlic pasta

1/2 pound angel hair pasta

2 tablespoons olive oil

3 large cloves garlic, minced

3 small pears, seeded and sliced 1/4 inch thick
(approx. 1 cup)

1/8 teaspoon crushed red pepper

Salt, to taste

1. In a large stockpot, cook pasta according to
package directions. Drain.

2. In a heavy skillet over medium heat, sauté the
garlic, pears, pepper, and salt in oil for 3 minutes.

3. Pour over pasta and toss to coat. Serve
immediately.

Yield: four 1-cup servings

FOR LIFE LOVE & FAMILY

FARMGIRL RECIPES
farmgirl
salad

FOR LIFE LOVE & FAMILY

farmgirl salad

1/2 cup fresh strawberries, sliced

1 small apple, thinly sliced

1/2 teaspoon lemon juice

1/2 cup almonds

1/4 cup fresh cilantro, chopped

2 cups mixed greens

1. Toss strawberries and apple with lemon juice.

2. Add remaining ingredients. Drizzle with Garlic Almond Vinaigrette (right) and toss.

Yield: four servings

garlic almond vinaigrette

1 small clove garlic, minced

1/2 teaspoon sea salt

2 teaspoons almond butter

1 tablespoon white wine vinegar

2 teaspoons honey

1/2 cup olive oil

In a pint jar, blend all ingredients and shake the jar vigorously for 3 to 5 minutes. Store, tightly covered, in the refrigerator for up to 3 days.

Yield: 2/3 cup

FARMGIRL RECIPES
farmgirl
muffins

FOR LIFE LOVE & FAMILY

farmgirl muffins

1 1/2 cups flour

2 teaspoons baking powder

1/4 teaspoon baking soda

3/4 teaspoon sea salt

1/3 cup plus 1 tablespoon brown sugar, divided

3/4 cup rolled oats

5 tablespoons butter

3/4 cup milk

1 teaspoon vanilla

1. Preheat oven to 350°F. Lightly oil muffin tins.

2. In a medium bowl, stir together flour, baking powder, baking soda, sea salt, and 1/3 cup brown sugar. Cut the butter into the flour mixture until it resembles small peas. Add oats. Make a depression or well in the center of the mix to receive the liquids.

3. In a separate bowl, stir together 3/4 cup milk and vanilla.

4. Pour liquids into the flour mixture. Beat with a wooden spoon for only about 15 strokes, until stiff batter forms. Do not over mix.

5. Fill muffin cups 2/3 full. Sprinkle tops with 1 tablespoon brown sugar.

6. Bake for 15-20 minutes or until golden brown.

Yield: six muffins

turkey & cream cheese sandwich

8 slices hearty whole wheat bread

1/2 cup cream cheese

1/4 cup sunflower seeds, toasted

8 slices smoked turkey

1 cup alfalfa sprouts

2 medium tomatoes, sliced

Salt and pepper, to taste

1. Spread cream cheese evenly over bread slices. Sprinkle with sunflower seeds.

2. Layer with turkey, sprouts, and tomato. Season with salt and pepper. Top with remaining bread slices.

Yield: four sandwiches

FOR LIFE LOVE & FAMILY

FARMGIRL RECIPES
farmgirl
soup

FOR LIFE LOVE & FAMILY

farmgirl squash soup

3 tablespoons butter

1 cup white onion, chopped

2 1/4 pounds (about 5 cups) butternut squash,
    peeled, seeded, and cubed

1/2 medium Granny Smith apple, peeled, cored,
    and diced

2 cups chicken broth

1 1/2 cups apple cider

1 1/2 teaspoons salt

2 teaspoons fresh thyme or 1/2 teaspoon dried

1/4 teaspoon black pepper

Sour cream (optional)

1. In a large stockpot, melt the butter over medium-
high heat. Add onion and sauté for 3 minutes.

2. Add the squash and apple to the stockpot and sauté
for 5 more minutes. Add the remaining ingredients
and bring to a boil.

3. Reduce heat to a simmer. Cover and cook for 20
minutes or until tender. Remove from heat.
4. In small batches, carefully purée the soup in a
blender or food processor until very smooth. Return
to stockpot. Serve immediately with a dollop of sour
cream.

Yield: four 1-cup servings

FARMGIRL RECIPES

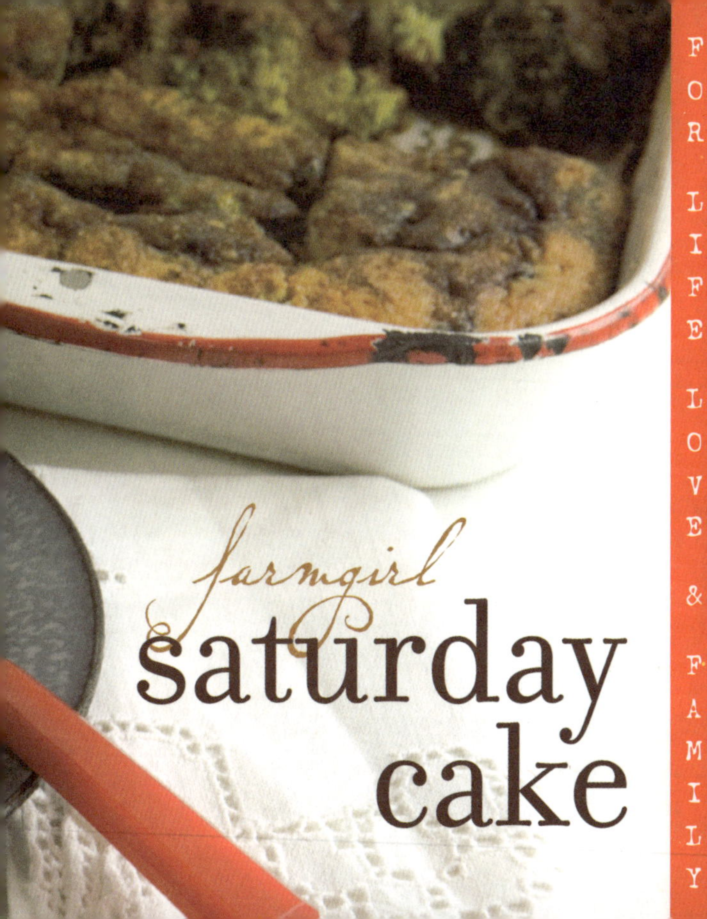

farmgirl
saturday
cake
FOR LIFE LOVE & FAMILY

farmgirl saturday cake

2 cups flour

1 1/2 cups sugar

1 teaspoon sea salt

1 teaspoon baking soda

1 large egg

1 cup buttermilk

1 teaspoon vanilla

1/2 cup butter, melted

2 cups fresh blueberries (or any other fresh or partially frozen berry)

Topping:

1/2 cup sugar

1 tablespoon cinnamon

1 tablespoon butter

1. Preheat oven to 350°F. Lightly oil a 9x13-inch
baking dish and dust with flour.

2. In a large bowl, mix together flour, sugar, salt, and
soda.

3. In a separate bowl, whisk the egg, buttermilk,
vanilla, and butter.

4. Add the liquid ingredients to the flour mixture
and stir until blended.

5. Fold in the blueberries. Pour into baking dish.

Topping:

1. Mix together the sugar and cinnamon. With
a pastry blender or fork, cut the butter into the
mixture and sprinkle over top of cake.

2. Bake for 30 to 35 minutes.

Yield: one 9 x 13-inch cake

DAILY MAKE DO CAN DO

MAMA says make it
do or do without

daily make-do, can-do
farmgirl
tips
FARM GIRL TIPS

DAILY MAKE DO CAN DO

❁ home care tip

Napkin Know-How

I grew up with cloth napkins, and I am always surprised when people don't have them. A good friend of mine showed me how to make some — very easy even for me, a non-sewer! Just cut large squares of cotton fabric and sew a narrow hem around the border. I now have a fun collection of napkins of all colors and patterns.

— *Sugar*

Fabric and upholstery shops are constantly discarding fabric sampler books, free for the taking. Bring them home and stitch up some napkins! (If there's paper backing on the fabric, just soak it in water until it lifts off.)

❧ garden tip

Think Butterflies

To attract butterflies, plant an abundance of flowers in a sunny location. They love echinacea, aster, cosmos, marigold, butterfly bush, zinnia, violet and phlox. If the area you live in is windy, build wind blocks and grow vines over them. Butterflies are delicate creatures that prefer calm, sunny days. You can also provide them with light-colored stones where they can bask in the warm sun and a bowl of water where they can drink. They love overripe fruit, so if you have fruit trees, you're in luck. But butterflies aren't the only ones you have to feed. Without caterpillars, there would be no butterflies, so be sure to plant food for them as well. They love dill, clover and fennel.

— Kate

FARM GIRL TIPS

DAILY MAKE DO CAN DO

🌸 personal care tip

Splinter Solution

The other day, I had a sliver so small I would have
needed a magnifying glass to remove it with tweezers,
but I sure could feel it. I grabbed a piece of scotch
tape, put it over the sliver, and voila, it was out!
— *Kim*

Measuring Up

Since I love to shop for antiques, I'm never without
a tape measure. I've learned to avoid the frustration
of not remembering measurements by sticking a
self-adhesive label to the side of my tape measure
for jotting down measurements and notes. I use a
pencil so I can continually erase the marks. After a
few weeks, I simply replace the label.
— *Connie*

✿ garden tip

Tricks for Tomatoes

The secret to healthy tomatoes is healthy soil. If your soil is rich and disease free, you will grow tomatoes with little effort. Rotating your crops every growing season, prepare soil for tomatoes by planting marigolds of the Golden Guardian or Tangerine variety to prevent or get rid of nematodes (microscopic worms in the soil) and till the marigolds into the soil after three months. And never plant tomatoes where you have recently planted other members of the nightshade family, like eggplant. To avoid tomatoes with cracked skins, pick them as soon as they ripen and before it rains.

—Devon

FARMGIRL TIPS

DAILY MAKE DO CAN DO

MURRAY & NICKELL
MFG. CO.
BLACK COHOSH
Cimicifuga Racemosa
CHICAGO, U.S.A.

GUARANTEED FIVE YEARS
CELLO
SANITARY & NOT
NATRA BOTTLE

❧ personal care tip

Elderberry Antidote

As far as herbal remedies, I swear by elderberry.
I usually use the capsules beginning in fall (one a
day) and drink elderberry tea from concentrates
if I can find it in a health-food store (must be
without additives or sugar). Just put a tablespoon of
concentrate in hot water and drink. When I take it
religiously through the winter, I never have gotten a
cold, sore throat or flu.

— Cecelia

❧ home care tip

Staying Stain Free

It seems like any dinner party you go to where red wine is served someone spills it on their new blouse, or a bite of cherry pie ends up in someone's lap. Try removing wine and fruit stains from linen by submerging the stain in boiling milk until it disappears.

To remove rust stains on white linens, rub the cloth with lemon and sprinkle with salt. Place in the sun, and the stain will disappear.

—Judy

FARM GIRL TIPS

DAILY MAKE DO CAN DO

❧ pet care tip

Natural Tick Repellant

I just read somewhere recently about the natural repelling properties of apple cider vinegar, and I've been using it to keep ticks off my cats and dogs. I simply apply a small amount to a damp wash cloth or paper towel and wipe my pets down every couple of days. Or it can be used as a final rinse during routine bathing. Use equal parts water and vinegar, and don't rinse — just let your pet air dry.

Another idea is to add 1 tablespoon organic cider vinegar per quart to your pet's drinking water. Gradually increase to a tablespoon. Adding gradually in small increments allows the digestive tract and your pet's taste buds to adjust.
— Paula

garden tip

Grow Your Own Vases

Next time you're searching for that perfect vase, look no further than your autumn garden. Pumpkins and winter squashes make beautiful, natural containers for your fall bouquets, worthy of centerpiece status on any table. And, once you've hollowed out the insides, put them in a collander and separate the seeds from the stringy mass. Then slow-roast the seeds in a cast iron skillet or the oven with butter and seasonings — beyond delicious!

—Julie

P.S. It's the ultimate in biodegradable!

FARM GIRL TIPS

DAILY MAKE DO CAN DO

🌸 home care tip

From Dryer Lint to Firestarters!

Recycle your dryer lint and paper egg cartons in a creative and useful way by turning them into smokeless/odorless firestarters. You will need dryer lint, paper egg cartons and paraffin wax. Save your dryer lint in a large storage bag. Once you have enough, press the lint tightly into the individual egg cradles in your paper egg cartons. Melt the wax on the stove in an old saucepan over low heat and pour it over the lint in the egg cartons. When the wax is cool, remove the "eggs." Your "egg" firestarters are waterproof, so they're great to take camping or backpacking. You can also use them in your indoor fireplace or wood stove.

—Kim

❧ farmgirl tips

And for the younger set (I *am* fifty-plus), I've included farmgirl tips from my "daughters," Kate and Meggie, who both work here at my farm. Kate (adorable as a speckled pup) is my soon-to-be daughter-in-law, and Meggie (whose beauty is as big as all outdoors) is my best friend. Born on the same day, five years apart (peas in a pod), they are the definition of "farmgirl sista'hood."

Farmgirl-stylin'

- Tie one on … an apron, that is!
- Carry a handkerchief and use it.
- Wear rain boots or cowboy boots in a color you don't normally wear — you'll look farmgirl fabulous!
- Wear charm bracelets in pairs, just for the sound of it!

FARMGIRL TIPS

"all gone"
Could I have another glass of that
Hires' Rootbeer?
COPYRIGHT 1894 BY THE CHAS E HIRES CO

✿ farmgirl tips

Gussy-it-up

- Shop garage sales, of course!
- Start a collection, any collection, and display it.
- Decorate liberally with rickrack.
- Display vintage postcards.
- Use embroidery hoops as picture frames.
- Use an untattered piece of an old quilt to cover your ironing board; make the rest into pillows.
- Use old cake stands or vintage bowls as plant holders and jewelry boxes.
- Use an old quilt to "reupholster" your couch.
- Collect old mirrors and hang them in a cluster, creating one large mirror.

❧ farmgirl tips

Gathered-up

- Use a chalkboard to announce your event or to label items on a buffet table.
- Use canning jars for glasses.
- Use glass gallon milk jugs for ice tea, and keep them covered with pretty vintage hankies tied with raffia or ribbon.
- Use galvanized washtubs to keep your bottled drinks on ice, or to stack dirty dishes in.
- Use mismatched vintage glasses and plates for table settings.

FARM GIRL TIPS

DAILY MAKE DO CAN DO

 farmgirl tips

Furnish-it

- Use an old door topped with 1/4-inch glass for a desk or table top (use two-drawer file cabinets for legs), or use a funky door as a headboard!
- Make side tables from old milk buckets or stacked suitcases.
- Replace your indoor pantry door with a pretty screen door, or hide an ugly bedroom closet door with a screen door and use it to display your jewelry (put it on hinges so it swings open).
- Suspend an old wooden ladder or toboggan above a kitchen island and hang your pots from it.
- Collect chairs in different styles and shapes to use around your kitchen table.
- Hide electronics in vintage cupboards — less metal and plastic, more wood!

❀ farmgirl tips

Make-it-do

- Make an apron out of an old tablecloth or sheet.
- For bulletin boards, glue old buttons, bottle caps or vintage earrings onto magnets, and display them on old washboards that hang on your walls.
- Use clothespins in place of office binder clips.
- Use bushel baskets for trash and laundry baskets.
- Store grains, beans, or rice in old gallon milk jars.
- Use cute vintage glass vases in your kitchen to hold utensils.
- Use pretty pedestal cake stands as candle holders or plant stands.

FARMGIRL TIPS

YOU KNOW YOU'RE A
you know you re a
farmgirl
when ...!
Campfire
Marshmallows

F A R M G I R L   W H E N ...

YOU KNOW YOU'RE A

You know you're a farmgirl when ...
your work and your play are the same thing.

You know you're a farmgirl when ...
"darning a sock" doesn't mean you're cursing it, just nursing it.

You know you're a farmgirl when ...
"Between hay and grass" is your daughter at age 12 (between childhood and adulthood); "go to grass" means "leave me alone"; and "eat hay" is your strongest version of "scram"; AND you know the difference between hay and straw.

You know you're a farmgirl when ...
an ear of raw sweet corn fresh from the stalk sends you right to the moon.

You know you're a farmgirl when ...
your purse contains a biscuit, hankie, crescent wrench, screwdriver, tape measure, fingernail polish, and fishing license.

You know you're a farmgirl when ...
you're more likely to be found in the barn than in the beauty parlor.
— *Aunt Jenny, Farmgirl Connection*

You know you're a farmgirl when ...
you sleep with your bedroom window open in the middle of winter.

You know you're a farmgirl when ...
"breakin' for a tune-up" means getting out your mechanic's tools, not your checkbook.

I DIG FARMBOYS
FARMGIRL WHEN:

YOU KNOW YOU'RE A

You know you're a farmgirl when …
the best part of your day is slipping into your mud
boots to head outside.
— *The Herb Lady, Farmgirl Connection*

You know you're a farmgirl when …
your "music" consists of birdsong, crickets, coyotes
(children of the night), wind gently rustling your
field corn, or a breeze rubbing the needles of your
"bull-pine" together.

You know you're a farmgirl when …
you'd rather sit around a campfire on a summer
evening than watch a movie.

You know you're a farmgirl when …
you refer to your "night waters" as "liquid household
activator" for your compost heap.

You know you're a farmgirl when ...

you get a wheelbarrow for your anniversary or Valentine's Day and say, "Just what I wanted!"
—*Aunt Jenny, Farmgirl Connection*

You know you're a farmgirl when ...

you make your birdhouses from junk you have laying around the "back 40."

You know you're a farmgirl when ...

as soon as you see a car pulling down the lane to your house, you instantly get up and make a fresh pot of coffee!
—*Nikki, Farmgirl Connection*

You know you're a farmgirl when ...

you head to your local library instead of doing a computer search, and "google" is something you do when you see a baby.

FARMGIRL WHEN ...

"When I was a kid, I played with duct tape. I didn't have a TV or Nintendo, so I made do with whatever I had. About twice a week, my mom would give me a roll and I'd invent everything from fly swatters to airplanes to wallets to snow pants!"
— EMIL (MARYJANE'S SON)

You know you're a farmgirl when …

"fire 'er up" means "makin' for town" in the grain truck, and "downsizing" is the month after Christmas.

You know you're a farmgirl when …

your romantic walk in the moonlight holding hands with your guy is the walk to the outhouse before turning in.

— *OwwLady, Farmgirl Connection*

You know you're a farmgirl when …

"neighbor" means someone who lives on your side of the ridge, but four miles away.

You know you're a farmgirl when …

an entire conversation with girlfriends revolves around hay.

— *Barn Goddess, Farmgirl Connection*

You know you're a city farmgirl when …

you sprinkle some bird seed near the "pond" that is the puddle of rain on the rooftop of an adjacent high-rise.

You know you're a farmgirl when …

you know what to do with thirty pounds of fresh tomatoes.

— *Susie Q, Farmgirl Connection*

You know you're a farmgirl when …

someone calls you an utter lunatic and you think they're referring to how "udderly" crazy you are about your milk cow.

You know you're a farmgirl when …

you leave the city and never look back.

— *Barn Goddess, Farmgirl Connection*

FARMGIRL WHEN...

MaryJane Butters, a woman of many aprons, discovered she was a writer when she needed a mail-order catalog for her line of organic foods, produced at her Idaho farm. When her passion for good stories got out of hand, her catalog became a "storefront" magazine (*MaryJanesFarm*), and eventually, she wrote a book sharing her message of simple, everyday organic living. *MaryJane's Ideabook, Cookbook, Lifebook … For The Farmgirl In All of Us* is now available in bookstores nationwide.

MaryJane grew up in Utah in a self-sufficient family of seven, longing for fertile ground where she could raise her own flock of chickens, maybe a cow or two, and a family. Working her way north, she made her living as a carpenter, waitress, seamstress, secretary, janitor, wilderness ranger, community organizer, and milkmaid.

Rooted now on her own five acres for the past twenty-one years (seven of those as a single mom), MaryJane has accomplished everything she set out to achieve, including a few surprises. Thirteen years ago, she married her neighbor, Nick Ogle, a third-generation farmer. Together they raised four hard-working children, plus bees, chickens, goats, cows, peas, beans, hay, wheat, and every vegetable imaginable, including a biodiesel crop to fuel MaryJane's car. She also created the "Farmgirl Connection," a website that brings together thousands of women sharing their farmgirl dreams and big farmgirl hearts, at www.maryjanesfarm.org.

About Cider Mill Press Book Publishers

Good ideas ripen with time. From seed to harvest,
Cider Mill Press strives to bring fine reading, information,
and entertainment together between the covers of its
creatively crafted books. Our Cider Mill bears fruit twice a
year, publishing a new crop of titles each Spring and Fall.

Visit us on the web at
www.cidermillpress.com
or write to us at
12 Port Farm Road
Kennebunkport, Maine 04046

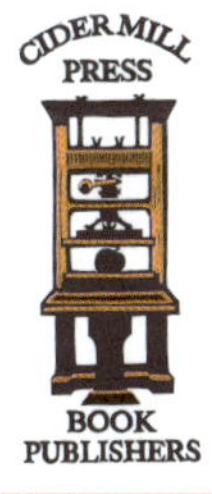

Where Good Books are
Ready for Press